W9-DAY-075
DISCARDED

THE COLLECTED WRITINGS OF WALLACE THURMAN